T0083868

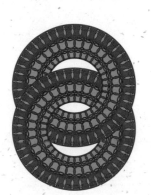

GRUB

Other Books by Martin Mooney

Bonfire Makers (1995)
Operation Sandcastle (1997)
Rasputin and His Children (2000)

GRUB

POEMS | MARTIN MOONEY

CavanKerry ❖ Press Ltd.

Library of Congress Cataloging-in-Publication Data

Mooney, Martin, 1964-
    Grub / by Martin Mooney.
        p. cm.
    ISBN 0-9678856-7-1
        I. Title.

PR6063.O586 G78 2001
821'.914--dc21   2001042505

Previously published by The Blackstaff Press,
Belfast, Northern Ireland.

Cover photograph: *Untitled* by Frankie Quinn
Author photograph © Star Black
Cover and text design by Pamela Flint

FIRST EDITION

CavanKerry Press Ltd.
Fort Lee, New Jersey
www.cavankerrypress.com

To Jacqui

CONTENTS

Foreword.. *xi*

PART I

Launching the whaler *Juan Peron* 3
Not walking, flying 8
The pastor's Sunday morning 9
The last showband 10
1941 11
...Gone for some time 12
King William Park 14
The man who ate crow 15
The fishermen 17
Angels 19
The fathers 20
Building an island 21
Windsurfers at Abbacy 22
Fleadh 23
Through the jazz window 25
Alice 26
For Charles Donnelly 27
The general secretary to his mistress 29
The anatomy lesson 30
Lee Harvey Oswalds 32
The General 34
A concert in Tbilisi 35
Anna Akhmatova's funeral 36
Among magicians 38
The mammoth 39
George Grosz 40
The Knowledge:
on not paying the poll tax 41

In the parlour 42
Not loving Irene Adler 43
A true history of Atlantis 45
Brecht in America 46
Men bathing, after Edvard Munch 47

PART II: GRUB

When did you last see your father? 51
Gate 49 53
Old Holborn 54
Pietà 55
Nocturne: Bow Belle 56
Nocturne: Calvi at Blackfriars 57
Aubade 58
Composed upon Westminster Bridge 59
Bathers 61
Glass 63
The chocolate grinder 65
Madonna and child 66
Odalisque 67
A journal of the plague year 68
The works 70
Ready-made 72
The expulsion of the moneychangers 74
Europe after the rain 76
The kiss 77
Nude descending a staircase 78
A last word from Roberto Calvi 80
A last word from Inspector Stubb 83
Wen 84
Landing 85

Acknowledgments 87

FOREWORD
by Baron Wormser

One mark of the genuine poet is the ability to revel in language and, at the same time, to query it. It's canny and uncanny; it's a high-wire act though the poet is the first to say that it's only words. Yet the poet knows how we live and die with those words in our grasping mouths. The poet treasures what is routinely disparaged but refuses to turn that treasuring into a self-righteous cause. Rather, the poet practices a sort of luminous wariness.

When I read Martin Mooney, from Northern Ireland, I feel there is no surface that his language could not pierce. Typically while he engages scenes that are far from conventionally poetic—a karaoke night, a pastor pondering his indifferent congregation, and, in his extraordinary long poem, an account of the down and out of drugged London—the descriptions he creates have a hard beauty that is acute and winning. He shows the reader how each moment of human life is fraught with menace and grace, as when he begins a poem entitled "Lee Harvey Oswalds" with "Marcel our Corsican barman handles the shaker / like a man playing the maracas. . .". We are alerted immediately and the subsequent edginess and boredom and looking-for-a-diversion rise from the opening moment like so much ruinous smoke from a casual fire. The reference to the drink is in earnest and is a joke just as the crazy energy of life and death that Lee Harvey Oswald manifested plays itself out in the persons of "three ageing survivors / of the world's greatest conspiracy, / who sit beneath a Coca-Cola sunshade / in their dark glasses and white suits / waiting for cameras or leggy girls / or cops, or anything at all." The last words may be a dying fall but they are hardly elegiac.

What steadily invigorates as one reads the poems is their unblinking intelligence. Mooney writes "History repeats itself, the first time / as tragedy, the second / as farce, and the third, perhaps / as poetry, condensing to syntax— / a beading, a softening, a transformation, / wings in the pupa, bone under the skin." Poetry is the skeletal yet sensual becoming that refuses to vanish. Behind the farce whose pratfalls echo the grave steps of history are the poet's stubborn words. Strong truths from often-harsh locales rely on the power of image to register themselves subtly yet fully.

Mooney's account of young people from Belfast adrift in amoral London at the end of the twentieth century is powerful and haunting stuff. Through a quietly masterful range of forms Mooney shows a number of souls sinking inevitably in a world that makes the seediness T.S. Eliot once observed seem like a nursery school. *Grub* is rightfully bleak but also shrewd and matter-of-fact as it notes how the wheels of crime and justice grind up some bodies just as other bodies manipulate the process or flee elsewhere. The epigraph for *Grub* comes from Jonathan Swift's "A Description of a City Shower" and in his poetic candor Mooney has everything in common with that great poet. *Grub* is unforgettable and this, Mooney's first book to be published in the United States, is a remarkable testimony to a poet who already has achieved much.

GRUB

PART I

LAUNCHING THE WHALER
JUAN PERON

When all that was solid melted into air
they were sixty feet above the frost
sparkling on the quay and on the water—
strung in the winter evening
like a new constellation.
Pure defiance buoyed them up;
to the insistent wheedling of gravity
their one reply was No Surrender.
Split seconds passed like hours
as the wind froze their faces
in the shapes of confusion
and their minds went backwards and forwards
unhurriedly seeking an explanation
for this casting-off of traces.

The April before, unseasonal showers
had blown from the northern hills.
As if nothing had changed
they could look down through the biting hail
to the scene below them, where
the Latin beauty on the slips isn't Evita
but her stand-in, Irene McClurg,
her skin almost the colour of shipyard tea,
her hair black as the looks
the foremen wear.
At half an hour's notice this secretary
from the electrical department
is launching the whaler *Juan Peron*
at the behest of the would-be guest of honour,
who has stayed at home

to be with her husband the dictator
in his trouble.
Eva, already plunging into history,
to tell you the truth the yard is happier
with this Protestant girl.
No Taig queen could raise a cheer
among these roughneck Islandmen
like Irene does . . .

The suddenly elevated, soon-to-be-dropped girl
stands with the dignitaries
among Union flags and handshakes.
In the South Atlantic,
between the Islas Malvinas
and Deception Island,
the whales keep to their ancestral
straight and narrow
in ignorance of the *Juan Peron.*
Born in Belfast,
part marvel of engineering
part slaughterhouse,
built to carry 24,000 tons of oil
from the bodies hauled up
bloody and howling into her dark interior
like a film of birth run backwards—
may God and Ulster bless her
and all who sail in her.

Irene goes home to Bangor.
The ship winters in the Musgrave channel
under the black hills. Deep-water
workers feel the cold eating its way

into their bones for ever.
Shouldering its superstructure
of winches, hooks and chains, huge drums
for oil, blades to shave the flesh
and blubber from the carcass,
all the arthritic machinery,
the *Juan Peron* plays host to hundreds
of the dunchered *crème de la crème,*
the lords of the kitchen house
and the frozen outdoor toilet.
It holds them to its bosom like a god.
It cherishes them like a benevolent king.

On the last day of the first month of the new year,
nineteen hundred and fifty-one,
with rationing in force and Brooke in power,
who saw in their ships
the hardiness, stiff-neckedness and stability
of the Ulster character,
sixty or seventy red-leaders and painters
mass on the top of the two-tiered gangway
that leads from the deck of the whaler *Juan Peron*
to the Musgrave quay.
They're talking wages, beer and football,
and when the wooden structure groans
someone who knows they shouldn't all
be there at once
cracks a bitter joke about a fall
and steps half off the deck, then wavers
with one foot suddenly in mid-air
for what seems like an hour.

Their bodies rain down
through the terrible scream of air rushing
from the severed vein of an air hose.
Some hit stone, others hit water
and sink like rivets
in the freezing channel.
Some hit the wooden fender under the hull
and the gangway slams down on their bodies.
Falling, they caught at anything.
One clutched at the air hose
and climbed back up onto the deck,
and one hung by his fingernails to a loose plate
for fifteen minutes. Most, though,
took hold of the nearest thing, the sleeve
of a workmate, as if two
would fall slower and land softer than one.
The injured lie scattered among bloodied caps
or are pulled from the water
with ice in their lungs.
The dead wait to be identified
by friends, or what was in their pockets.

Two pages back, after the small advertisements—
Smart Boy Wanted . . . Room To Let
Close To Shipyard—
broken lines and arrows chart their fall
from the *Juan Peron.*
The survivors talk
of walking in space, of escaping
with cuts and bruises,
of being, by the Grace
of God, delivered;

and shown in close-up,
the gangway hangs
like a fractured arm in a sling.
Everything's askew.
The tide brings eighteen caps upriver.

NOT WALKING, FLYING

She shuddered in her seat, for someone
was walking over her grave, or over
all of their graves at once. Outside,
night leapt away from them
and the earth with its few lights
rushed up. A man across the aisles
prayed at the top of his voice
as if his God was an elderly gent
gone utterly deaf. Don't shout,
she wanted to say, be patient.

For her God was suddenly visible.
He lived in a white bungalow
with a flag and space for two cars
under its hacienda arches. Fields
rolled away to knots of trees, the pink
cream of the motorway's concrete
matched by the blossom on his hedge.
He came out onto his long drive
and smiled, he was her neighbour,
and though he kept guns in the house
her children went to school with his
and he would look after them.

Another tremor: a tiny sky-quake.
Not walking, flying: something
had flown over her grave, its wing
taking a blade of shadow to the grass.

THE PASTOR'S SUNDAY MORNING

Dressing in darkness, my starched collar
crackles with the static of the Word.
November rain lashes the tabernacles,

and daybreak bristles with scripture
from Harland and Wolff to Iron Hall
like redbrick spires above terraces.

My guilty double, the fat publican,
crosses the street for his Sunday papers.
His arteries brim with cholesterol . . .
I am shaved red-raw as a pig's cheek.

The cars arrive in coats of turtle wax.
(If only Grace was wax and sin water . . .)
My big-boned flock are dressed to kill.
I will take up a silent collection.

THE LAST SHOWBAND

Another karaoke night . . .
a dance hall on a northern coast
(condemned, three-quarters empty) rings
to our 'Testing, testing . . . One . . . Two . . .'
The crap night that set this curfew's
no worse weather than filled houses
before the Japanese invented music.
Once we swept folk off their feet
into the blizzard from the mirror balls.
Now we play to the poor sweepings
of this jukebox statelet—six
schoolgirls, seventeen OAPs,
Old Flames and Honky-tonk Angels—
all romantics, all incurables.

1941

My grandfather manned the ack-ack . . . Coming
home late, he would fish for his door key,
reeling it up on the end of its string.

When the Luftwaffe knocked on the door
and then walked in without waiting
like a neighbour come to borrow sugar,

dust and debris swam in the blacked-
out hall; but halfway up the stairs,
key, string and letter box lay intact.

...GONE FOR SOME TIME

I could tell our chances were slim.
The bottle of Scotch on the flag-draped table
hadn't been touched, the water was gone,
the atmosphere was frosty, Anglo-Irish, polite.
The winter moon was a sliver of ice
from Captain Oates's eyebrow, when the man
himself stood shivering at the mantel,
white as a stag night flour-bomb victim.

'Eighty years, and the same circumlocutions.'
The voice was Ulster via Sandhurst,
a schoolmaster's finally broached patience:
'Why did I ever try to set an example
to people so literal-minded? Your frostbitten
loyalty, your sleepwalking in circles
was not what I meant.' I coughed. Robinson
muttered 'Lundy', and the dam burst . . .

'It's time you followed in my footsteps.
Expose yourselves to the elements, let
blizzardy Antrim's gale-skewered plateau
confront you with yourselves, like Lear—'
And then as if by way of illustration
he vanished in an explosion of bad weather,
blown roof slates, torn umbrellas, snow,
the door wide open like an invitation

to table-talk in white and formal rooms,
a kind of eighteenth-century heaven
bathed in the glacial light of Reason . . .

Suddenly something scattered the mirage
and all that was left of where we'd started from
was the wind howling over a set of prints
that led away from an ice-stiffened flag,
dead dogs, a tent buried in drifts.

KING WILLIAM PARK

Flat on my back in the dead roses, I tried
to outstare the full moon's Sabbatarian
eye, and failed. Conscience is blackout—

the Rigger, my father, does my remembering,
dead-drunk in his neglected grave. At least
his guess, or anyone's, is as good as mine.

Little Alice was a victim of the cold war—
I swigged my brother's vodka and I shrank
and withered till I looked like a Methuselah.

When the barman barred me with a curse
I was the drink-witch who hexed his clientele,
plucking the Tampax from up under my skirt

—that was when the bastard called the police—
and chucking it among the lunch-time crowd.
I was the shit who threw bleach in his face.

Daybreak's a throat scald, aftershave or schnapps.
That white eye hasn't slept a wink all night.
Memory's a baby cancer trying to grow up,

a skin graft or a transplant that won't take.
In daylight almost everything says DRINK ME.
The moon's policemen batter me awake.

THE MAN WHO ATE CROW

When they took away the children
my ghost of a wife wept
for a week and a half. The room
I'd painted pink and scattered
with an ark of animals
went grey-haired overnight,
so I roamed the town, haunting
the gates of all the schools
until someone said, 'Go home,
you frighten the kids.'
I frightened myself. I taped
cardboard over the window
my wife had broken,
then I bandaged her wrists
in one of my old work shirts,
which reminded me of work,
collecting my cards,
and spending hour on hour
in a crumbling office hurling
dog's abuse at an empty desk.
When I borrowed the 12-bore
from a drunken hunter
he must have thought I meant
to do harm to someone,
so he called the police,
who battered down my door
that winter morning
as I dressed. A woman officer
put an arm around my wife.
A tall man with a moustache

wrinkled his nose at the pot
where one black feather floated
among the stringy meat.

THE FISHERMEN

Half four. Long-distance fishermen
keep their pre-dawn pub-made appointments.
A car idling, a door bell, a car door slammed,
the noises lift like bubbles in the dark
to high-rise windows.
Shift workers' lights come on,

freezers glow in shopping malls,
headlamps find signs:
south and west, the sun behind the car.
Farms shrink behind hills.
At six they pass an accident, slowing
through a chicane of traffic cones,

a slewed green armoured car,
an ambulance, troops and police,
a body on a stretcher . . .
'Poor fucker,' someone says. 'Speed kills.'
The driver keeps his foot down for a mile
then leaves the motorway

and finds the river half hidden in reeds.
They cast and brood on water,
fanned out along the bank
like a search party. Nothing bites,
the morning's long as life,
and one by one into all of their minds

swims the idea of the river bottom
and the one uncaught ancestral fish

that's there for the taking,
the reptilian hide, the scale-sheathed
gangrenous eye in the silt,
the mouthful of hooks.

ANGELS

The children we don't have already have names
they will grow up resenting . . .
Angels in supermarkets, their favourite reading
is Shakespeare, Fielding and Marx.

They are already immune to religion,
middle-class piety, tantrums and sulks,
Oedipal rage, and the urge to be poets.
For my part I'm almost the perfect father.

In bed with their mother, I address them
like small, invisible adults,
but to them I'm an object of derision—
feckless, pointless, crippled by risk,

half catatonic with money worries and fear
of failure, and deaf to their screams:
'Hurry, it's urgent. Get it over with now.
Let us get you out of our systems.'

THE FATHERS

They are so much older than us
that they live only in photographs,
where they crowd the pavements
or jaywalk between tramcars.

We barely recognise them, whose
shirts are without collars
and whose waistcoats are chained
to their own buttons—

they are all strangers in suits,
as if every day was a Sunday
where you keep your cap on
and worship the god machinery.

Even today old men, their sons,
preserve their hand-me-downs,
keep faith with pocket watches
at well-attended funerals,

raise old-fashioned hats to wives,
widows, roomfuls of daughters,
their heads full of old street maps
and the long-culverted rivers.

BUILDING AN ISLAND

The art of playing god has come down in the world.
Yesterday these men were boys
being taught the rudiments of the pre-Copernican
universe, its spheres and epicycles
and its hidden engines. Today
they are driving bulldozers and dump trucks
at the edge of a shrinking sea,
they work in a hurricane of gulls,
building an island.

Underneath them, layers of stone
quarried from the demolition sites of the world,
abandoned hospitals, offices
left empty by an exodus of secretaries,
schools whose students have gone
on the children's crusade
into one or other of the forbidden zones.
Underneath that, in turn, the bones
of sea fish fossilise.

After their long migration from the mainland
lifeforms tense and breed.
Evolving new strains, adapting to circumstance,
they will learn to graze
these miraculous flatlands.
Tomorrow the building of houses begins;
already a kind of grass grows on the surface
between the tin cans and oil drums
leaking slime.

WINDSURFERS AT ABBACY

Their empty cars lie parked up on the grass
and near the roadside. Latecomers,
one in a wet-suit, are tugging a sleek board
to the shingle, its hinged mast
a thin bone broken. Others

have already taken wing,
their sails triangular and taut as eardrums.
They swing like radar dishes through
the small crises of the shallows
towards the sunlight's Morse, the deeper water.

FLEADH

The barmaid that night in the Phoenix Bar
was staggering drunk
and dreaming of California.
Her American friends
were 'over for the festival,
doing a bit of theatre'—
All's Well That Ends Well—
or was it *The Quare Gunk*?

She was the best of mates with half
the musicians of Ireland,
had kissed all of The Dubliners
and thought of Christy
as the son she never had.
Had they all pissed in the back yard,
I wondered, holding my breath
till we made it outdoors.

And how did she stand with the poets?
'Oh wild Willy Yeats and me
go back a long way:
it was him give me the black eye
you see in the snapshots.
I still have the very slate
we kept for Behan.
And,' she beamed, turning,

'do you see that in the jar?
That's no pickled egg,
but what's left of Kavanagh's lung,

the one they removed for cancer.
He gave me jar and all
one night outside the dance hall.
Thank God it wasn't his leg,
he was a great dancer.'

THROUGH THE JAZZ WINDOW

for Kevin Smith

I'd had so much sun I was well stoned,
suddenly Samuel Taylor Coleridge
with his head in a sling, taking
himself on a day trip, everyone else
for a ride. Even the jazzmen
were digging their rhythms out of
pure light, till sunburnt music
blew in smoke rings from the window.
'Imagine a pathway. Describe it . . .'
This one follows the railway lines
from one tunnel to the next, set
in landscaped parkland with
a city on the horizon. 'Now, what
does that tell you about yourself?'

Nothing, except that I remember
how once this hour of the afternoon
would have been time for *Playschool*
or *Tales of the Riverbank,* and
that through the jazz window today
no one has gone or is going to work,
preferring instead their own
company or that of idle friends,
and one foot, the big toe bare,
sticks way out over the sill like
a housewife talking to neighbours
or a long solo being improvised
to the astonishment of strangers,
describing a pathway . . .

ALICE

The house in Donnybrook Street was a hive of draughts,
cold infesting the long crack in the skirting
and the hardly imaginable space below the floor;

that first winter, a lace curtain of frost
on the inside of your windows brought you under
my quilt and three blankets for the first time,

where to put out your arm was to run the risk
of frostbite, and to sleep with a cheek exposed
was to dream of a visit to the dentist . . .

For the first time we went through the looking-glass
chapter by chapter, me reading, you dwindling
quickly to sleep, up to your eyes in bedclothes,

with Alice no longer the little girl she was
and my voice like the idiot grin of the Cheshire Cat,
still hovering inexplicably over your head

muttering 'curiouser and curiouser' to itself.

FOR CHARLES DONNELLY

I
What's stranger than a poet in battle,
and yet less strange?
Nothing more natural than the hard
tack of a rationed language,
the slogan, the death rattle.
So perhaps you were almost at home,
as if the loyalist lines
were the broken strings of a fiddle,
and the crackling of gunfire,
the spray on the deck of the steamer
making the crossing to Spain,
nothing but a shower of hail
clattering down on the tin roof
of a barn near Dungannon.

II
I could light up a comradely cigarette
or pass a bottle,
asking in return only a word or two
of pidgin Spanish, enough
for a folk song, a love song
and a conversation.

Or, instead, to be read letters from home,
until the uncharted distance
between County Tyrone and Madrid
is mapped and populated:
This be the Kingdom of Prester John . . .
Here be dragons . . .

III
And here, at the arse end of nowhere,
a collage of posters
is being soaked to a pulp, the words—

what's left of them—worth more
than the paper they're printed on,
now the ink is seeping . . .

History repeats itself, the first time
as tragedy, the second
as farce, and the third, perhaps

as poetry, condensed to syntax—
a beading, a softening, a transformation,
wings in the pupa, bone under the skin.

IV
The camelopard is the giraffe of the imagination,
a kind of unsuspected flower
still sealed in the brown paper of the bulb
in our eight by four of garden;

the centaur is a kid on his father's shoulders
on the outskirts of the estate,
heading into the long history of their town.
The plan of the city streets

is spreading like lichen on stone,
or like nerve fibres, recolonising a wound
impossibly. Under its grey skin
the rhinoceros is becoming the unicorn.

THE GENERAL SECRETARY
TO HIS MISTRESS

You are so much more than any conceit,
my dacha, my little epaulette,
my medal-ribboned 1950s overcoat.

For you I'd give my place on the podium,
my Zil limousine, my fur hat.
My hard currency's at your disposal.

O my little republic, my buffer state,
the thought of your secession
has frightened me out of my wits.

Just promise we'll stay close together.
I'll send you my soldiers and tanks.
Our standing ovation will go on for ever.

THE ANATOMY LESSON

He has opened the envelope of the arm
and drawn out the red letter
like a forceps baby, gingerly
as he'd stitch a slashed wrist
or defuse an unexploded bomb,

and looks like a conjuror, pulling
yard after yard of silk scarves
the colour of wet capsicum
from his sleeve, or a string
of scalpel blades from his mouth.

Meanwhile, anaesthetized behind him,
like someone watching Christ
slicing bread and filleting trout
to feed the five thousand,
I can't help but wonder

whose cadaver that is, turning
its nose up as if at the smell
of its own decay—being
dissected like arguments for
and against the existence of God.

It might be my own, strung up
for stealing an old overcoat
only the day before, and already
the colour of house dust—
which is, after all, mostly skin.

Am I watching my mortal remains
being put to good purpose
for the first time in my life?
And do any of these rotund burghers
feel the hair on their heads

rising to the occasion
while Tulp unravels my fibres,
warp from weft, untangles
vein and artery, muscle and sinew
like live, earth and neutral,

or feel me standing among them,
somewhere between dissolution
and a kind of immortality,
craning my stiff neck
to learn from my unveiling?

I'm as keen to be put in the picture
as any member of the guild,
and just as full of admiration
for the skill of the surgeon,
his dexterity with the knife

between my wrist and my elbow,
like that of the scribe with a pen
or the lover with fingers—
like nothing else in the world,
a matter of some certainty.

LEE HARVEY OSWALDS

Marcel our Corsican barman handles the shaker
like a man playing the maracas—
even at our table at the edge of the street
we hear him crushing ice. He is as proud
of this his own invention as you might
be of a brilliant child, and grins
as he pours it into three long glasses
crazed by hours in the refrigerator.
Sugar, rum, vodka, tomato juice, blue
curaçao, bitters, green chartreuse . . .
'Three Lee Harvey Oswalds comin' up, boss,
just the way you've always liked them.'
The same routine, the same flourish
of olives and tiny parasols, lemon
and salt, as well as the same broad smiles
from the Arab con man, the African boy
who sells his foil-wrapped dice of hash
in the alley under my verandah,
and from the fishermen playing poker
at the farthest table, for the life jackets
none of them ever wears. Hardly on more
than nodding terms, I know a name
or two, and some of them call me Papa
after Hemingway, so often pretending
I've taken them into my confidence
that I'm bored with the rumours they spread,
saying I traffic in heroin, or arms,
that I shot the president . . . The same
mad stories, as if fiction could save us
from heat, lethargy and the small crimes

that make up life, as if gossip
was worth more than truth in the end,
when the winds come north from Morocco
and the city bakes, studying itself
like one of the three ageing survivors
of the world's greatest conspiracy,
who sit beneath a Coca-Cola sunshade
in their dark glasses and white suits
waiting for cameras or leggy girls
or cops, or anything at all.

THE GENERAL

Because today is Sunday and there is no war
to keep him at his desk, the General
has taken time off to come out in the sun.
Even so early the park is crowded
with men in shirt sleeves like himself:
his friend the Admiral sails a fleet
of paper battleships across the pond,
a Major of their acquaintance sags
in a deck chair near the bandstand, as
musicians from his regiment play
the themes from all his favourite movies,
The Dambusters, A Bridge Too Far. The General
finds himself whistling 'Colonel Bogie'
as he strolls among the tanned civilians,
happy to let them lie there unconscripted,
all maps and strategies forgotten,
no coups and no conspiracies to plan.
He smiles, and the sun smiles back at him
from the glass towers of the financial district,
whose windows hold the image of a kite
that someone somewhere else is flying.

A CONCERT IN TBILISI

They toured the world but always came home
with their own music ringing ironically
in their ears. It was the eldest brother
who deciphered their dream of America:
a speakeasy in the Latin quarter,
torch songs, moonshine, a tobacco-mist
cut to ribbons by their émigré jazz.

Boarding the aircraft, they carried guns
instead of their instruments, spinning
a yarn about a concert in Tbilisi
before demanding: 'Fly us to Chicago.'
Broiling on tarmac, they had them dancing
in the aisles. The mother jammed
with a shell-shocked Afghantsi
who hugged his guitar like a dying comrade.

ANNA AKHMATOVA'S FUNERAL

It looks to me like a hero's welcome,
as they carry you on their shoulders
to the grave, with no more delicacy
than they would cheap furniture,
like a slender matchwood wardrobe
full of old clothes and coat hangers
or an incomplete dinner service
packed in shavings and newsprint.
If I took it at face value I'd say
the untidiness of it all sits easily
with poetry, suggesting a life
lived according to nobody's rules
among messy bookshelves, tables
buried under an avalanche of drafts
in a house that's a home for anyone
who happens to knock on the door.
In the kitchen a pan of milk boils
over, smoke burps from the samovar,
a month's salads turn bitter . . . And,
in the same way, you might never
have bothered to dress yourself
or put on make-up, to answer letters
or pay the bills. The ragged edge
unravels back from the graveside
into any number of possible lives,
each one less orderly, less disciplined,
and already, so soon after them all,
history is learning to ignore you,
despite the presence of the film crew
and the mourners, who might as well

be spectators filling a stadium
or the night shift on its way home.
Admit it, it has its attractions, this
rough-handed slovenliness of things:
you could slip to one side unnoticed
and watch, suppressing a smile
that says, 'How light she is, how easily
they hold her up above their heads,
no heavier than a child or a poem,
no more solid than the priest's sermon
or the crumbling laws of gravity.'
Weightless, you tiptoe backwards
out of the cemetery, like a shy guest
still distrusting her invitation,
go home to any of the lives you led
without leaving so much as a thumbprint
or a stray eyelash to be picked up
by the unsteady gaze of the camera
skirting the edge of absence.

AMONG MAGICIANS

We have opened up the charmed circle.
We are accessories to shrinkage.
Our horizons narrow to domestic props
(coins, twine, safety matches, hankies)
or to rhinestones and blue one-liners,
either the strip club or the work top.
Of course, those evening-dressed nostalgics,
yesterday's masters of the big gesture,
sword swallowers, spoon benders, escape artistes
are still dropping themselves in deep water,
but jiggery-pokery, the alchemists
are as rare as Marxists. Our last trick
is the Indian rope trick, with the rope
pulled up after our vanishing ankles.

THE MAMMOTH

Bitter and twisted, the verdict said:
I was a Trotskyite with an axe to grind
on Art's whetstone, and deserved no better.
Let him paint tundra. The judge's laugh
was the snicker of wind in the crunchy
grass when some poor zek's mattock
turned up a nugget of iced steak.
A handful of cynical Old Bolsheviks,
we stared at each other, afraid of hope,
then bent our backs to the excavation
of the earth-snared bulk in the permafrost
whose shoulders wore a matted shawl
of hair like sisal. Like food's granny
history lay there, rigorous but unrationed.
Eating it still frozen was like chewing
glass embedded in putty, but it thawed
in the mouth gradually, weeping blood
and enzymes. Forgotten meat-juice,
Bruegel's Cockaigne: we puked and crapped
our second helpings, hoarded cutlets
in our shirts, felt flesh against the skin
under our arms, where it was warm . . .
Dragging my feet through the camp gates
I savoured the reek from under my collar
of our carcass measured in banquets,
our arctic larder and bottomless cook pot
already sweating its brown meltwater.

GEORGE GROSZ

This man is a bone stuck in the world's throat.
His tuxedo is festooned with cigars.
His girlfriend is as thin as a fish-hook.

This man is little more than a torso and a head.
His eyes dress always in bandages.
His sons and daughters are derelict houses.

This man believes in electricity and scalpels,
crutches, gramophones, venereal disease . . .
His fists are full of hypodermic needles.

THE KNOWLEDGE: ON
NOT PAYING THE POLL TAX

I was two years in the Irish colonies.
My London-Irish cabby was an amateur
actor with a Dickensian greed
for anecdote. He'd drunk with Behan,
met O'Casey, had the Knowledge:
a man or woman with two surnames
might get you a room in a Hendon squat
or a sublet council flat in Neasden.
An envelope marked TO THE OCCUPIER
was my marching orders, the television
pined for the permanence of showrooms.
From Camden to Cricklewood Broadway
the curtains in every gaff were furred
with the soot of old tenancies
and every new kitchen was smeared
with a coat of yellowish grease.
The oily ash below the fridge, charred
fat baked into the walls of the oven
were voices whispering in Cockney:
Krook, Krook, Krook . . . You go up
like a candle with your bones for a wick,
only your boots and hat survive.
Everyone has to cough up in the end.

IN THE PARLOUR

'Every connection is a revelation.
People I pierced and tethered secretly
always dreaded the giveaway clink:
now that's all out in the open. Look
in the portfolio, towards the back,
for a picture of the man whose penis
has been sliced lengthwise, the two
halves of the glans like segments
of dusty purple fruit, pinned by metal.
You can't see it but the gold
ends in an anus-ring. That's his wife,
the skinhead Aphrodite overleaf,
her clitoris bound to her nipples,
nose and navel, as if she thinks
the insurrectionary body might break up
and break away, escape from itself
into a Balkans of erogenous zones . . .
In the last photograph they stand
face to face, chin to brow, the space
between them bright with chains.
Leaning backwards, they hold each other up.'

NOT LOVING IRENE ADLER

As a lover, he would have placed himself in a false
position . . . To admit such intrusions into his own
delicate and finely adjusted temperament was to
introduce a distracting factor which might throw
doubt upon all his mental results.
Arthur Conan Doyle, 'A Scandal in Bohemia'

Tonight I inhale
Bach violin concerti,
indoor gunfire,
the newly electrified
city streets,
fine porcelain, bone meal—
all grist to my mill.

A frenzy of high notes
climbs the stairs
to an insomniac
crescendo. A month's
uneaten meals
are a penicillin farm.
I have snow in my face.

'. . . Whatever is left,
however improbable,
must be the truth.'
I was never myself
when we met,
absorbed like sugar
in damp lanes,

my head full of secrets
and empires,
the chill mathematics
of suicide chess
and corruption.
I was a connoisseur,
a skeleton

in a long overcoat,
and felt you,
when I worked late,
a shadow-boxer
ducking my punches,
a deep-water shoal
always escaping my nets.

'To be left till called for . . .'
The thought of you
is gas lamps in thick fog,
aurora borealis.
At the open window
the night sky is lobster
and turquoise

like a foreign postmark.
Your photograph
collects a fur of ice
in a locked drawer.
Like everything else
in the world, my eyes
are freezing over.

A TRUE HISTORY OF ATLANTIS

We've discovered the truth—
no island city. Instead
a federation of shipwrights
and sailors. Sea nomads

whose currency was gen,
whose politics dealt in description,
the whereabouts of timber,
citrus fruit, fresh water.

They prized: honesty.
Accurate maps. Mensuration.
Physical strength. Good eyesight.
They worshipped the whale.

In council every fourth year
clans becalmed in debate
heard their elders marking
how the ice encroached,

how error crept into charts
like forgetfulness, a glacier
that mobilised armadas . . .
The survivors brought ashore

intricate knots and a taste for salt.
Mythological islands
and swamped peninsulas.
Names like *Jonah* and *Noah*.

BRECHT IN AMERICA

We sailed from Siberia, and when I testified,
I was more than halfway
through my circumnavigation,
an enemy alien who was an enemy
and an alien everywhere.
Christ, what a cliché!

Somewhere, in somebody's headquarters,
Weigel's phone calls are taped
and some agent's wife is listening
to her old recipe for goulash
in the original Polish.
Once she even went out to their car

and invited the G-men inside
for a cup of coffee . . .
Another continent, another railway . . .
Franz Kafka, you were half right
in your ultimate city,
but what you never saw

was that single track
cutting a whole country in half,
arrowing into the sun . . . Let me tell you,
you can forget everything but home
and will do or say anything
to get back there.

MEN BATHING,
AFTER EDVARD MUNCH

Their wet heads are jaggy as pine cones
opening to sunlight on the sill
of the brightest room in the house;
the surf's coarse marbling
is the work of an apprentice painter
learning to woodgrain doors,
a trial piece in trompe l'oeil
that deceives no one.

Shin-deep,
they are wading out of the sun
as if out of a factory,
each neat, chilled penis cradled
in a nest of wet pubes
like the shell in the *Birth of Venus.*

PART II

GRUB

Now from all parts the swelling kennels flow,
And bear their trophies with them as they go:
Filth of all hues and odour, seem to tell
What street, they sail'd from, by their sight and smell.
They, as each torrent drives with rapid force,
From Smithfield to St Pulchre's shape their course,
And in each confluence join'd at Snowhill ridge,
Fall from the Conduit prone to Holborn Bridge.
Sweeping from butchers' stalls, dung, guts and blood,
Drown'd puppies, stinking sprats, all drench'd in mud,
Dead cats and turnip tops come tumbling down the flood.

Jonathan Swift, *A Description of a City Shower*

WHEN DID YOU LAST
SEE YOUR FATHER?

Inspector Stubb of the Yard
has more on his mind
than you'd guess from his eyes,
those steamed-up mirrors
in the wall of his face.
For instance, an explanation
of a death in custody
so hot on the heels of his part
in the Stalker débâcle,
it makes him shudder.
And in Willesden Green—
Little Limerick.
He mulls a cover-up, a lost
pathologist's report, a lie
or two strategically placed
in Murdoch's papers:
say, he drowned in his own
puke, his lungs filled . . .
A shoal of red herrings
swims through his head
as he knocks back cold coffee
at a table on Broadway.
The motive appears to be
robbery . . . There may well
be an Irish connection . . .
That Sir Alfred was chosen
for this brutal slaying
was a tragedy not just
for his family and friends
but for British democracy . . .

His eyelids droop, the shoal
darts electrically off
into uncharted waters, away
from the shark, Truth:
the Honourable Member
was known to associate
with thieves and addicts
and paid for their favours,
the beatings and fist-fuckings,
in coarse white powder.
Stubb smiles, knowing the price
such stories fetch
on the open market,
and he strolls to the park
to shape his sentences
at the edge of the water.

GATE 49

If air's the poet's element each poem's a landing,
sometimes an effortless, perfect touchdown,

more often endangered and delayed. Circling
above Heathrow, peering out at landmarks

I recognised from TV and the tourist circuit,
I rehearsed my sonnet for the Special Branch,

all names and addresses. In my pocket
a sheaf of directions mapped a mock-epic.

My ears still rang as I was questioned:
'What is the purpose of your journey?

'Where will you be staying? And who with?'
I might have answered: self-imposed exile;

terra firma; with the other Irish losers—
unlikely though. They let me through

and onto the tube, where the green suburbs
led to the worming maze below the city

and to Victoria Station, the concourse
a huddle of rucksacks and beggars

like a scene from a famine or a lost war.
'Any spare change . . . homeless . . . hungry . . .'

The voices were always over my shoulder.
After each landing, the interrogation.

OLD HOLBORN

Grub's coked out of his mind on the underground.
There are no more commuters, the drunk
and the dangerous, the hardened and devil-may-care
are the only ones braving the tiled halls tonight
as Grub's band, The City Reptiles,
cut all too perceptibly from the last bars
of their thrash cover of 'The Soldiers' Song'
to a reverent 'Anarchy in the UK'.
Since the last time the cops moved them on
his coal-under-the-door voice has gone
the way of all flesh. Now his whispered
croaks are drowned by feedback
but no one else knows or remembers
a word of any of the songs they sing.
Grub is the brains behind the band.

Grub is the brains behind the band,
even if he hasn't a single answer
to the questions hanging over his head:
all he has in his seventeen pockets
are the odds of his last Giro,
an out-of-date rail card,
a few desiccated fibres of Old Holborn
and a chunk of stone, a souvenir
of the death by suicide of Roberto Calvi.
Coked out of his mind, he reckons
some day this stuff will come in handy.

PIETÀ

They carry him via the off-sales to the squat,
throw him down on somebody's mattress
and undress him. As he sprawls like a god

they unlace the calf-length oxblood Docs,
unstrap and peel off the three layers
of slashed and fraying bondage trousers

like a month-old bandage on a wound.
They raise him, gently, and draw up
the cutaway denim and the black tee shirt.

There's a red tattoo under the left nipple
and fading bruises all over his rib cage
from a kicking doled out in a boozer.

He opens an eye. Sinéad swims into view
climbing uncarpeted stairs in bare feet,
already stripped down to her underwear.

Too stoned to stay awake, let alone fuck,
he goes under as she climbs on top,
and dreams of being a splinter in her heel.

NOCTURNE: BOW BELLE

Slow heave of water   the liquid breath
of an animal   asleep in darkness
some river-bed   carnivore.
You can feel it   dream of massacres
whole herds slaughtered   at the crossing places.
Breeds sleep   this tug and loose
this cradle-rocking   muscle.
Makes drowsy   flex and relaxation.
We concentrate   on lights and buildings
moorings and bridges   destinations
we have passed down   through families.
Lambeth. Westminster.   County Hall.
Tower Bridge.   Traitors' Gate.
Billow and fall   billow and fall.

NOCTURNE: CALVI AT BLACKFRIARS

Weighted with half-bricks like a rioter,
I still hang from the bridge:
the tide has gone out under my nose
a thousand times; I dangle
over mud again tonight.

I stink of its black stew
of bicycles and kitchen scraps,
rotten pigeons, oil, sewage.
There's no substitute for candour:
I reek like Judas the suicide.

A rat up on its hind legs sniffs
where a bare foot swung,
then slithers off. The empty air
is sour with old vendettas
grown stale and overfamiliar.

I'm a victim of my loyalty
to the implacable machine
that pegged me here to dry.
Betrayal and retribution
were two cogs meshing perfectly.

Even at mole-blind midnight
the noise is deafening—
there's work if not cash in conspiracies.
Mud-gas belches like a glutton,
old trenchfoot-breath, my master.

AUBADE

Those that have jobs get up for work;
someone manages a coffee, someone else
performs the miracle of eggs and bacon,
someone barfs noisily into the sink.
A knock-off ghettoblaster blares the news—
murder in Belfast, drowning on the Thames.
Grub sleeps through everything, and dreams.

COMPOSED UPON
WESTMINSTER BRIDGE

The fifty-one dead dancers of the *Marchioness*
waltz through Grub's babbling stupor.
They tumble tidelong, bumping into bridges:
brother Lycidas, brother exile, brother leper.

They mumble, 'All we did was live
according to the ways of the city, enjoying
the slow alcoholic sway of the river,
the thousand lights upon it. Now, dying

'(for what? carelessness? somebody's profit?),
we've joined the lights beneath the water,
bloated, blurred, and dissipated . . .'
The Thames's sons, the river's daughters.

Grub catches on: 'Fuck sake!
Your rhyme's an insult, your tidiness
lets profit and the system off the hook.'
It's the first time he's addressed me,

even in sleep. 'Christ, has this century
taught you fuck all, or what?
Half a hundred party animals like us
swallowed up by Party City's river,

'its big brown sewer, its shit-stream,
and here you're putting words into their mouths.
Face facts and make others face them:
it isn't verse that's on their tongues

'but glar and shite and chemicals
and weed and glass and water
where there'd been beer and gin
and the makings of a long French kiss.

'Be clear, man. They were victims.
They wouldn't talk like this.'

BATHERS

Stubb doesn't like to brood
on the sex that simmers
just under the surface
of his orderly city . . .
a slippery confusion
of limbs and genitalia
behind the façades.
Sometimes it looks as if
everyone's bedding everyone
else, in a huge orgy,
a black hole sucking
the guilty and innocent
into its whirlpool.
As he feeds the wild geese
of St James's Park
he likes to pretend
that it's not happening,
that things are the way
he wants them to be.
His perfect world
would be like the park,
a space for citizens
between palace and barracks,
a uniformed band
playing to sunbathers.
Still, it's under control
and it can be useful
to scatter the titbits,
to let people catch
a once-in-a-while glimpse

of a famous thigh . . .
It keeps them amused
and out of trouble,
it keeps them, implausibly,
almost happy.

GLASS

Annie works in a pub. Sinéad sells rubberwear
and used pornography in a tiny shop
it costs an hour's wages to enter. Joe Cancer,
the Reptiles' drummer, is unemployed.
He follows his nose to Camden Town
and bums the price of a Special Brew.
His fellow travellers work the streets
like salesmen, intimidating and polite.
Grub wakes up and hits the streets as well,
cruises Victoria (worse than useless),
rides the Circle Line for hand-outs
('Spare us some change, mate . . .'),
then comes up from the underworld again
feeling dizzy, seasick, fragile . . .
Like a job-hunter, he rehearses
his curriculum vitae: an A level in art,
summer in Europe, winter at home,
then a wet spring on a building site
sweeping floors and sleeping rough.
The first band formed at sixteen, the first
chords came almost a year later
for the school hops and youth club discos
that came to nothing. The guitar
was sold to an off-duty Brit in Stranraer
for a fortnight's beer and roll-ups.
Dole from May to July, hiding in the Tate,
meeting Sinéad under the *Large Glass,*
unleashing one another on themselves
beneath that flawed copy. She found the squat
and on their first night in its attic

tattooed him with red ink and a pin,
a tiny rose and cross . . . He's near the river
when this train of thought pulls up.
Next stop Shanty Town. Somewhere between
RPG Avenue and the Sydenham bypass
Belfast coughed them up and spat them out—
himself, Annie, Joe, Sinéad, crossing
in ones and twos in their thousands,
life stories taking a turn for the worse.

THE CHOCOLATE GRINDER

Annie rubs polish from the plumbing:
there's the stink of piss, a crusty
scale of dried-up phlegm or vomit
that has to be scratched from the copper
with a wire brush or a fingernail.
The rag picks up a black smear
that soaks through onto the hands,
making the skin look dry and grey.
She thinks, most men would be disgusted by
this girl with the hands of a corpse.
Not Joe, he doesn't seem to mind
He of all people knows the score.
In bed he's wary, needs to be told
who's boss—something to do with
the men who rent him by the hour.
Oh she knows about it, worries
about AIDS, about the Vice Squad,
but it's money. And she trusts him.
It makes more sense than the pub grind
from eight in the morning to midnight
sometimes, being snitted at, tipped,
tried out, exhausted, underpaid.
At least he's there at night to talk to,
drink and get stoned with. She likes
their sessions in the early hours.
The mad shapes of sex and music
loom through a fog of Brasso.

MADONNA AND CHILD

I bump into Grub on the Embankment,
sharing a flat pint bottle
of watered-down cough mixture
with a derelict Irishwoman.
He coughs and hawks a greeting.
She screeches 'Up the Ra',
and wrecks their nest
of cardboard and newspaper.

I recognise her woollen overcoat
and the thin summer frock
worn under a back number
of the *Irish News.* Her plastic bag
says Stewarts, not Safeways.
When Grub leers and snuggles close
he's enjoying my confusion:
she could be his granny or his lover.

'I was looking for my mother,'
he says. 'A last resort . . .
I haven't seen her since I was nine,
so for all anyone knows
this could be a family reunion.'
He licks the cracked brown leatherette
stretched over her cheekbones
and a cord of spittle links them for a second.

ODALISQUE

A punter's leafing through the magazines.
Sinéad's aware that he's convinced
she's watching him. Expectant, timorous,
his eyes flick towards her, then away,
like a fly's orbit round a light bulb.
She knows by now he'll spend the afternoon
waiting for the moment he can lock a door
on the pair of them, dressing her
in the wild outfits of his imagination:
the strapped and buckled plastic, studs
and gas masks, thongs and hoods.
She'd like to hurt him and he wants her to.

A JOURNAL OF THE PLAGUE YEAR

I
August: a rainstorm as violent as it is sudden
sweeps London Bridge like an epidemic,
a wet pox catching everyone by surprise.
On mobbed doorsteps umbrellas bloom
with a metallic rustle, an insect noise,
a roach-click.
        Soaked to the skin,
Grub scuttles into Southwark, where the sun's
already fumigating the cobblestones
under the archway of the George Tavern.
By the time he appears in the doorway
of the back room where I'm sitting—
a snivelling, raggedy silhouette—
the wet courtyard shines like a coin.

Inside it's still the sixteen hundreds,
I've a tankard of ale, a bench,
the parliament clock to tell the time,
and a dark corner. He startles me,
this blinking croppy, this time-traveller,
this postcard from the nineteen eighties,
and snorts at my alarm.
              'What, afraid
of catching something?'

II
'All right, you're safe. I'll stay here,
and you can stay in isolation.
We could get you an oxygen tent

and a lover in gloves and a mask,
like in that film, *The Boy in the Bubble*.
So maybe sarcasm is the lowest form
of wit, but you should see your face.
Die like that, you won't get buried.

'Anyway, I'm sorry I slagged your poetry.
I'd like to show you some of my songs
sometime, see what you think.
That's what you should do—songs
about what's really happening, you know.
If I didn't think they'd infect you
I'd introduce you to my mates, the band.'
He contemplates the window's

fish-eyes of steamed-up glass.
'Think we'll see more rain? I hope so,
it's what this town needs after
the heatwave. Do you know "London Calling"
by The Clash?' He draws nearer.
'You should write poetry like that,
something everyone could take to,
something to set the town on fire.'

THE WORKS

Everyone tells time in their own way:
Annie by the sunlight on the bar,
Joe by the drawn-out ascent of his beer
and charley high, then the time bomb
of his comedown starting to tick . . .

Grub blinks up at a stain on the ceiling
with the regularity of the metronome
he'd wanted on the cover of his first
album, *An Object to be Destroyed* . . .
Now he doesn't even want the album.

Lifting a fiver from the till, then ten,
Sinéad glances at her wristwatch.
The case is transparent, the works visible.
Half past four. The manager's down
in the basement go-go, drunk and horny.

Grub blinks up at the ceiling . . .
We're drunk on politics and spleen
and bashing Thatcher with rolled-up copies
of his *Class War,* my *Socialist Worker.*
He hasn't said a thing in half an hour

when suddenly, 'It's time I hit the road.
It's been great crack, but it wasn't real.
Stick to your hackwork and satire,
be foul-mouthed, lumpen, and obscene,
but don't expect anyone to take notice

'unless you hit a raw nerve. Here, take this—'
He chucks a wad of crumpled foolscap
on the table, downs his dregs, and leaves before
I read: *London's Burning. Grubsongs.*
They're beer-stained and almost illegible,

scratchy hieroglyphics, dog-eared verses
full of anger and the spiky friction
of the fantastic and the everyday.
Words for music perhaps, but I can't imagine
the tunes they could ever be set to.

READY-MADE

Joe Cancer's just
what the doctor ordered

for this pinstriped Tory
in the white Merc

whose meditations
are full of birch.

He asks Joe's name
and what he charges;

Joe names a price
and then himself:

Holy Joe, Joe Soap,
Joe Ninety,

Little Joe, Jo
the crossing-sweeper . . .

then nothing's said
until they reach a flat

where it's all scripted
like TV wrestling,

a punishing schedule
of belts and blows,

crime and punishment,
the short, sharp shock

of penetration,
the waves of excitement

like angels dancing
at the tip of the needle,

like a maiden speech
getting a standing ovation:

thayhonnerrubbleginnlemin . . .
It seems impossible

to go too far.
Joe does.

THE EXPULSION OF
THE MONEYCHANGERS

Grub and God's banker run into each other
on a Stop The City demo: the one
hotfooting it from a cop on a horse,
the other rolling his eyes like a fish
with a sense of irony, taking it all in.
The Monument's Protestant sundial
inches a shadow towards Pudding Lane.

The mountie pulls up. Grub's vanished
up some side street or into a car,
he thinks. He clops back to the riot,
away from Calvi's sphere of influence
and invisibility. *'Buongiorno,'*
the Italian greets him. On second thoughts
it's less a greeting than a question.

'How goes the day? Are you winning?
How many policemen have you hospitalised?
How many cars have you overturned?
Have you managed to mug
the Doddering Old Bitch of Threadneedle Street—
or isn't that the correct translation?'
His sarcasm can't hurt Grub,

who sees a club tie and stick pin
and goes for the jugular. It dissolves.
'Ectoplasm. As insubstantial as credit.'
Grub flails until he's exhausted.
'Don't waste your anger,' says Calvi.
'You can't win, and trying to beat us
this way, you actually join us.'

To catcalls and whistles from the Square Mile
Grub tries to resist the hypnotic
singsong and lash the boot in. 'Get fucked.
I hate your sort, I want to see you die—'
('Too late,' says Calvi.) 'You can't channel
anger,' Grub gulders, 'you can't control
anarchy—' ('By definition,' smiles Calvi.)

'I haven't forgotten your business
with the bomb in Bologna station.
I know your kind, and your kind's friends,
always from the far right of the spectrum.'
'Not always, anyone angry will do—
you, for instance, or your stoned flatmates.
Apart from which, I'm history now . . .'

It's getting dark, and Calvi has to go.
Squad cars and ambulances whoop
like hunters on a scent. Grub, small,
tired, and undernourished, effs and blinds
at empty space, and isn't sure.
Was it a waking dream, or too much hash?
He sways back to the skirmish

meaning to stay well out of trouble
till he can shake the nagging doubt
that something grim is going on.
Ghosts and dreams—a bad sign.
This enemy up from the underworld
is after something. This banker
wants his earmarked pound of flesh.

EUROPE AFTER THE RAIN

As far as Joe's concerned, this train
could be taking him anywhere.

His head is singing, holding the one
deafening, high-pitched note

and the ads for Heathrow and Gatwick
play lurid variations

on the theme of escape. He broods
on all the likely destinations:

Amsterdam, Paris, Copenhagen
or New York. Even Belfast.

The names melt like flesh in acid
into a single, surreal haven,

not *my cock between those thighs*
or the candle stuck in his arse

that looked like a stick
of gelignite, slippy, weeping . . .

Says Joe to Annie three hours later,
I think I killed the fucker.

THE KISS

It's dark before Grub makes it home—
he remembers seven snakebites in the Crown,
then crawling between the cement boots
of four-and-twenty Tipperary men
who heard the accent, saw the skinhead,
put two and two together and got Shankill.

Joe and Annie stumble in, kissing.
Joe mutters that they've found a party
and invites him. But it's a long, long way
from Cricklewood to Mayfair when
you're bruised and drunk, and friends
whose names you don't remember disappear

to make mysterious, anonymous phone calls.
And now Grub's having trouble getting up
from the hall floor where they left him.
He's sick. The nightworld whirls
and here's a cop, now two, now four,
a vanload, spinning lights . . .

NUDE DESCENDING A STAIRCASE

Night after night
                    Sinéad weathers
the city traffic
                    cops and kerb crawlers
madmen for Jesus
                    sad Rastafarians
lonely hearts.
                    The galleries
close at eight
                    portraits and landscapes
hug their alarms.
                    She envies the man
who peppered the Leonardo
                              his clarity
and sense of purpose.
                              Vague and mute
she scratches sleep
                    in damp corners
dreams of Grub.
                    Now he's dead
she can't imagine
                    how they lived
how they made love
                    when everything
was under water.
                    London's drowning.
Thames swallows Clapham
                              the traffic lights
blink like buoys
                    cars run aground

on submerged rocks.
                    In a council block
the lift is fused.
                    She climbs
twelve flights
                    to reach dry land.
Floodwater rises.
                    Before it reaches
her graffitied lair
                    she plans to swim
for the distant island
                    of Highgate
knowing she'll tire
                    halfway.
An army helicopter
                    long-lost harpy
probes the flotsam
                    with its searchlight
and loud-hailer
                    begs for survivors.
She stays hidden
                    until the time comes
to creep downstairs
                    to the water's edge.
Opening a window there
                    she dives
and doesn't surface.

A LAST WORD
FROM ROBERTO CALVI

When I meet Grub for the last time
it's with Calvi down in the wreck
of the *Marchioness,* among the tables
and chairs and overturned glasses.
It's like the aftermath of a bar brawl
in some B western, where everything
was made of balsa and polystyrene.
'It might as well have been,' croaks Grub,
massaging his livid throat, 'for all
it took to sink her. Fucking disgrace.'
Calvi coughs, looking ill at ease
in the less-than-salubrious company
of a dead punk and a crazy poet.
'Anyway, remember me to Belfast
and to Sinéad, if ever you two meet up.'
I haven't the heart to tell him.
'I know, looking back, that what
we had together wasn't much, but
it was all we had. Ask Joe and Annie
why they set me up. Otherwise, say
you never heard tell of me.'
Calvi's treading water, impatient.
I'm about to ask what's behind
this new friendship, when God's banker
volunteers a strangled explanation:
'Class warfare is like any other;
it makes traitors and scapegoats,
strange bedfellows and reluctant allies.
Grub and I were mercenaries. Now
we want to pay everyone back.

Don't you believe in ghosts, Mr Mooney?
You must admit they have their uses.'

The stove-in timbers suddenly lurch.
The wreck's being winched up to begin
the body count, with a dull rattle
and throb of chains and engines
on the surface. Already crowds
of tourists stacked like angels in an icon
are blocking traffic on the bridges.
The ghosts release themselves into the current
and Grub nods to his wordy countryman
before he vanishes into the murk.
Calvi's goodbye takes longer. Drifting
away through a lopsided bulkhead,
he snarls, 'You're an intelligent man,
don't think that he and I have more
in common than a seedy martyrdom.
He's the scum of the earth, the waste
product of the social machine
and it's hell to be stuck with him,
but this will go on, with people like Grub
forever pushed to the sidelines
and beyond, with people like yours truly
strung up for going too far
in the right direction. Remember—'
The bulkhead gulps air and Calvi
is wrenched out into the stream,
farting 'capitalism' and 'propitiation'.
And I am sucked to the surface, where—
among the babble of the mourners
and the hiss of flashcubes, and taken

either for a corpse or a survivor—
it's the easiest thing in the world
just to disappear . . .

A LAST WORD
FROM INSPECTOR STUBB

Stubb clears his head
with the *Telegraph*'s
crossword and obits,
the dead colonels
still spluttering
under their monocles.
He takes for granted
their English outrage,
he puts it in his pipe
and smokes it . . .
It's my last afternoon
in the Buckingham Arms,
Little Sanctuary,
I've packed my bags.
Stubb offers a last pint
and a lift to Victoria
with a shrug of his shoulders:
'No hard feelings . . .
the first casualty
of war is truth. It caught
a blighty one this time,
but with your help
we preserved order.
Will our story hold water?'
He's a plausible man,
so it's just possible.
He taps out his pipe
and we trot to his Rover.
It's bucketing down.

WEN

The memorial service for Sir Alfred X
fills one of the last Wren churches
with the furled umbrellas of the age.
Across the road in a wet alley Joe
Cancer looks like a bomb's hit him—
a consumptive Dickensian gnome, his
Mohican singed to a yard-brush
badger-stripe, the black hole of his gob
issuing wisps of smoke or steam.
'Annie's gone. The Reptiles are finished.
Old contacts avoid me like the plague.'
A reflex cadging palm and then a head-shake.
'What happened? I was half pissed
in King's Cross and had to take a leak
on the line. Imagine the fireworks—'
Arc light. Rainbows. Little lightning.
The cops thought he'd been blowtorched
by some feminist vigilante, another
who'll never be cured of the Great Wen.
He spits out a mouthful of char and walks
off, disintegrating slowly in the rain.

LANDING

Annie is crossing the United States,
learning to breathe oxygen again.
Sleeping with senators and delegates.
The fresh air's rushing to her brain.

The open spaces and the city streets
lend their exhilarating spin
to all her senses. In her thoughts
her brave new world is blue and green.

It races up, a map of lights
she'll follow to its brightest town,
a bank account, a crop of noughts.
This is how new lives begin.

ACKNOWLEDGMENTS

Some of these poems have previously appeared in *Fortnight, Gown Literary Supplement,* the *Honest Ulsterman, The New Younger Irish Poets* (Blackstaff Press, 1991), *Poetry Wales,* the *Review, Rhinoceros* and the *Rialto.*

A NOTE FROM THE PUBLISHER

CavanKerry Press regularly reserves a place on its calendar for publishing out-of-print books that deserve permanence. Bringing *lost* books back to life is core to the CavanKerry ethos and in this way, we honor the work of the writer.

—*Joan Cusack Handler*